COLLECTING

*H*ARLEY-
DAVIDSON

CARL CAIATI

Alliance Publishin

This book is not sponsored by the Harley-Davidson Motor Co. Model names, designations, and some photographs lent for publication are copyrighted by Harley-Davidson. Official Harley-Davidson trademarks are used for identification purposes only. This is *not* an official Harley-Davidson publication.

629.2275
C12c
Copy 2

ISBN 1-887110-14-3

Design by Cynthia Dunne

Alliance Books are available at special discounts for bulk
purchases for sales and promotions, premiums, fund
raising, or educational use.
For details, contact:

Alliance Publishing, Inc.
P. O. Box 080377
Brooklyn, New York 11208-0002

Distributed to the trade by National Book Network, Inc.

10 9 8 7 6 5 4 3 2 1

CONTENTS

CHAPTER 3
Harley-Davidson Collectible
Memorabilia

CHAPTER 4
Instant Expert Quiz

This book is dedicated to the legendary Phil Peterson, Harley dealership owner (Phil Peterson's Harley-Davidson, Miami, Fla.), Harley-Davidson enthusiast and rider, respected colleague, and the epitome of congeniality.

ACKNOWLEDGMENTS

We must first bestow earned laurels to all the fine people who assisted me without reservation on this select project.

First and foremost, the great and revered Harley-Davidson Motor Company and its first-rate publicity department. Profound gratitude goes to the Harley Archive director, Martin Jack Rosenblum. Always available on the phone, Marty provided me with all the assistance and time he could muster, and for his unstinting cooperation I am extremely grateful.

Again I must commend the Harley-Davidson public relations team for providing me years ago with a cornucopia of Harley-Davidson stock motorcycle photos, which are a permanent part of my research file and my own personal and treasured collectibles. With their permission, I was able to reprint them in this concise mini-manual, greatly enhancing the visual aspect of the book.

Harley-Davidson dealers, old and new, also ably assisted and to them I offer a vote of appreciation.

Personally, I would like to thank other individuals in the Harley sales and aftermarket field. Reynold and Rocky of Brothers III allowed me to photograph some rare and unusual items: motorcycles and other collectibles. Sonny Steel ditto! A fine gentleman, Sonny provided much collectible material for examination and photographing from his U.S. Steel shop.

Last, but never the least, Phil Peterson of Peterson's Harley-Davidson, Miami. Phil, a revered and respected colleague, gentleman of the highest caliber, true and veteran biker, allowed me to photograph his fine collectible vintage 1928 motorcycle, a pristine restoration. Phil is not only a Harley person, but a part of the Harley legend.

In closing I must also thank The Franklin Mint for providing me with photos of their magnificent Harley-Davidson replicas, which are jewels in their own right and destined to become rare and coveted Harley collectibles.

Carl Caiati

CHAPTER 1

HARLEY-DAVIDSON AND THE MOTORCYCLE MYSTIQUE

The Harley-Davidson phenomenon has become a part of the American culture, encompassing a lifestyle that has been embraced by a multitude, from lawyers, doctors, and associated yuppie types right down to the common workingman.

As American as mom's apple pie, the Harley-Davidson motorcycle (the ultimate cruiser), with the eagle and extended wings logo adorning many past and current models, has become legendary over the years, creating worldwide motorcycle subcultures and an aura known as the "Harley Mystique" around the two-wheeled idiom.

A classic example of the American corporate dream and success story, belabored by foreign competition and financial obstacles, the company persevered until it pioneered and manufactured an internationally acclaimed, desirable product that proved to be a rare quality American product.

The first Harley-Davidson motorcycle emanated from a Milwaukee, Wisconsin, shed so small it was once picked up and carried by hand. In 1903, three Davidson brothers—Arthur, Walter, Sr., William—and one William S. Harley founded the company. It was a gutsy move at a time when personal transportation was in its infancy. Would the world ride, let alone buy, the two-wheeled equivalent of a horseless carriage? The fledgling outfit soon had its answer: Harley sales grew steadily, and the firm soon established a reputation for advanced engineering with a 1912 racer sporting four-valve heads when mere balloon ties were considered an innovation. By 1926, sales mushroomed to 23,354 units.

In 1929, Harley debuted the first in a long line of twin-cylinder V engines that still remain the heart of its product. Three 45-cubic-inch V-Twins ranged from a low-compression D model for sidecar and three-wheeler application, to the standard DL offering, to the higher compression DLD.

The next watershed year for Harley was 1936, with the introduction of a 61-cubic-inch V-Twin that had features highly advanced for its day. Nicknamed the "Knucklehead" for the distinctive shape of its valve covers, this powerhouse featured a then-revolutionary combination: overhead combustion chamber and fully recirculating oil system. Another major improvement was a six-plate clutch with alternating steel and fiber inserts and spring control for smoother, more positive shifting. To convince the few doubters, the factory built a streamlined, knuckle-powered racer that shattered speed records with ease. Harley enlarged the engine to 74 cubic inches in 1941, giving rise to an advertising phrase, "Big Twin," that aficionados still affectionately call their Harley motorcycles today.

The year 1948 found Harley improving the breed again, and ahead of its time. The new 74-

inch Panhead engine superseded the Knuckle with a new all-aluminum cylinder head, plus widespread use of the light alloy throughout for substantial weight savings and heat dissipation. A key to such innovation was Harley's commitment to vertical integration. Except for carburetors and tires, everything on their motorcycles was made in their Milwaukee factory—from sparkplugs to spokes, from gas tanks to gaskets, from pistons to pushrods. For decades it was a unique advantage. Harley's detailed engineering improvements stood in stark contrast to Detroit's preoccupation with annual cosmetic styling changes. And in 1949 they were at it again, introducing hydraulically damped telescopic front suspension in their Hydra-Glide model. Harley brought hydraulic shock suspension to the rear of the frame in 1958 in the form of the new Duo-Glide. Curiously, their 1957 model remains a collector's item. It was the only year with a rigid frame that had the cleaner-appearing straight front bars of the Duo-Glide.

Meanwhile, the first in a wave of challenges to Harley's domination of the American motorcycle market—and ultimately, its very existence—had begun. H-D had surmounted economic hard times before. Sales had plummeted by over half in the early 1920's due to a postwar slump and increasing acceptance of Henry Ford's low-cost model T. And just as recovery loomed, the Great Depression struck. Harley aggressively cut output by 80 percent by 1933, down to a bare bones 3,700 motorcycles. Management earned widespread admiration for keeping Harley from going under; one of the rewards was lucrative government business during World War Two. Harley even fielded a new machine designed for use in the war, the opposed cylinder XA. Postwar performance riders came to prize XA forks because their longer length gave a few precious inches extra in cornering clearance. Ironically, this latest test grew out of that war. GI's returning to the U.S. from overseas came home with a preference for many imported motorcycles:

Triumphs, Zundapps, BSAs, BMWs, Nortons, Moto Guzzis. For many riders, less became more. They were smaller, lighter, peppier, and most importantly, less expensive.

The rise in import popularity, especially Japanese machines, took its toll among Harley riders, allowing foreign firms to gain a foothold in the American marketplace.

The trend grew slowly but inexorably, and soon claimed its first casualty. The Indian Motorcycle Company, Harley's main domestic competitor, had over the years also placed its bets on large touring motorcycles. It was the first to respond and the first to founder. Indian fielded a new line of lightweight vertical single- and twin-cylinder models, the Arrow and Warrior. But they failed technically, and by 1953 Indian ceased making its own motorcycles. The victims weren't just in America. Vincent, which built a powerful British V-Twin with legendary speed exceeded only by its sky-high price tag, went out of business in 1955.

Because of the quest for lightness and speed, many Harley buffs began taking weighty frills off their bikes, altering the machines and their aesthetics to emulate the image of the imports. Helping the situation was the easy parts interchangeability of the Harley models. Entire books have been written on what fits what in different Harleys. It was possible to build a better Harley by selecting the cream of many years and incorporating it into a more select, ridable machine.

Around 1950, California speed merchant Chet Herbert concocted another notable early custom, the Beast, a stripped-down Knucklehead. It was enlarged to 80 cubic inches by using stroker flywheels cleverly adapted from Harley's obscure UL model and sported dual carbs on custom-brazed heads. It was like something out of *Ripley's Believe It or Not*. This two-wheeled terror bested a U.S.A.F. P-80 jet fighter during a highly publicized drag race. The only thing on two wheels that could touch it was another dragster aptly named Double

Trouble. This was a Triumph with not one but two full race engines; these custom-modified "bob-jobs" or "choppers" were the birth pangs of a vibrant aftermarket for lightweight, high-performance, and customized Harley parts. Today it has grown into a multimillion dollar industry. Magazines like *Easyriders* and *American Rider* cater to Harley riders and builders exclusively. Harley customizers like Ron Finch, Dave Perewitz, and Arlen Ness have styling clout to rival automotive legends like George Barris and Roly Fernandez. And parts choices are so extensive that it is possible (though expensive) to build a motorcycle completely from aftermarket parts—crankcases, frames, con-rods, wheels, cylinder heads, oil pumps, the whole nine yards.

In 1954 bigger things began to happen in H-D's Milwaukee headquarters. Harley went back to its roots to create a new, compact junior twin, the K-Model. It was a radically revamped version of the old 45-inch series that had started the V-Twin dynasty. Of particular note was a new crankcase that contained the transmission and primary drive in one unit with the engine—a feature almost a decade ahead of the competition. So solid was this engineering base that race versions (such as the KR) Harley really answered the imports with the potent and lean Sportster, an evolution of the K-model with 55 cubic inches, overhead valves, and magneto ignition on many models. Its lean, spare design was a significant departure from the Big Twin, which had oversized everything to benefit the touring rider—tires, wheels, fenders, saddlebags, forks, and gas tank. No slouch in performance either, the "Sporty" was cleverly geared for retina-detaching acceleration over a city block. Such was the Sportster's success that variants are still being turned out today, ranging from a 74-cubic-inch XLH to a no-frills import fighter, the 883 c.c. XLX.

The XL's owed their unexcelled performance to their responsive overhead valve systems, which made them power potent. The 1958 Sportster mills even added performance virtuosity incorporated into the F and X series. Changes for 1962 included short, staggered dual exhaust, and the fork brackets and motor mounts were refashioned in aluminum. In 1964 aluminum front wheel hubs became standard on all Sportster models. In 1965 the electrical system was upped to twelve volts. In 1968 the hot XLCH Twin was capable of producing 58 hp at 6,800 rpm. The front fork was again altered to upgrade handling. The change from a dry to a wet clutch was made in 1971 in order to simplify timing adjustments, and the timing was set into the cam cover. In 1979 the XLS roadster appeared with low rider styling, fitted with a 16-inch rear tire. A KL "hugger" model offered lowered seating via shortened shock absorbers. In 1983 a no-frills XLX was offered as well as a limited production XR-1000. Up to and including 1985 Harley-Davidson offered three Sportster models: the XLX, XR-1000, and the regular Sportster, all of which featured an improved, upgraded 1000 c.c. motor. In 1986, the XR-1000 was dropped from the roster, superseded by the new Sportster 1100 XLH. Also premiering that year was the 883 c.c. Evolution powered XLH, replacing the XLX.

Meanwhile, Harley went on perfecting the tried and true big brother. A new "Shovelhead" design emerged along with electric starting in the mid-1960's, the Electra-Glide. In 1978 the design was again enlarged to a monstrous 80 cubic inches and output topped 60 horsepower. But storm clouds were brewing in the market again. In 1963 a new entrant targeted American shores with the now-famed "You meet the nicest people on a Honda" ad campaign. It was a veiled and underhanded swipe at the Harley rider, who was by implication somehow mad, bad, and dangerous to know. (The Honda ads contributed to a macho Harley image that would later return to haunt Honda.) But it was a new marketing approach. For decades, Harley had occasionally struggled, often thrived, but always survived by primarily selling motorcycles to diedin-the-wool motorcyclists, the military, and loyal police departments across America. Honda was trying to enlarge the entire pie by persuading the penny-loafer and sweater crowd to try two wheels. For a while they and other Japanese vendors sold mostly small sportcycles—hardly a threat to H-D's domination of the heavyweight segment.

By 1969, it was another story. Many Japanese-initiated riders were now ready to trade up. And Honda was ready. They fielded a smooth, powerful, and sophisticated 45-inch four-cylinder machine. Slowly but surely the flood gates opened. Driven by domestic demand, big bikes of all descriptions had begun to flood America from the orient. By the late 1970's even Harley's distinctive and unique features were being cloned—the hairy-sounding, aircraft-like V-Twin engine and comfortable cruising seat position that had given it a lock on the long-distance touring market for so many years.

Harley somehow coped for a while. In 1971, they fought back with the Super-Glide. It was a cut-down, simplified Big-Twin, and the biggest styling departure since the Sportster. But in the midst of the marketing crisis, the company was hit by a bigger thunderbolt; it was acquired by conglomerate AMF. For decades a small, closely controlled company, Harley now had a parent and a bad case of corporate culture shock. The Japanese continued to make inroads throughout the 1970's with fresh, reliable, low-priced machines—the result of a long-term commitment to quality and productivity. Meanwhile Harley's internal problems seemed to be leading it in the other direction. AMF infused the company with cash, but a priority was placed on production numbers at the expense of research and development and inspection control. In AMF's defense, federally mandated environmental rules required a heavy investment in sound and emission control programs. But the company also alienated long-time loyal employees by abruptly pulling up the stakes of their manufacturing operation and depositing it in York, Pennsylvania. During the dark days of the early seventies, there were rumors of sabotage, hardly assuaged by quality control problems. And H-D's price disadvantage ballooned. Even loyal customers began to depart in droves. For a while the crisis rose to such a magnitude that few thought the desperately ailing company would survive.

Eventually some of AMF's charges began to take positive effect. And inside Harley itself a new name, Willie G. Davidson, began to be mentioned as someone who listened to customers and was willing to break with Harley's rigid past. Beginning with the 1979 Low Rider, a growing variety of sporting models based on the venerable Big Twin and the Sportster began to roll off the assembly line. Thanks to Willie G.'s influence, at long last you could buy a customized model—albeit conservative—right off the showroom floor.

After a decade of ownership without any clear turnaround, however, AMF began to make noises about selling. Formerly American Machine and Foundry, AMF had acquired Harley as part of a strategy to transform themselves into a colossus in the leisure-time industry, with products from Voit basketballs to Brunswick bowling alleys. It appears they may have overreached themselves by adding motor vehicle manufacturing to their stable. Whether the acquisition by AMF helped or hindered Harley-Davidson is a matter of controversy, but if they hadn't stepped in, Harley would have most likely faced an early demise.

One economic instrument that could help the ailing company was a tariff. A tariff would serve to boost the competition's prices and eliminate a glut of import inventories overhanging domestic sales. The ITC placed a substantial import relief tariff of up to 45 percent on all Japanese motorcycles of 700 c.c. or more displacement entering America. Along with the nearly 50 percent drop in the yen-to-dollar differential, it put Harley on equal footing at last. And this outcome dovetailed beautifully with a new, aggressively focused approach at Harley—go after the heavyweight cruiser market exclusively. Harley discovered it possessed other advantages as well. Situated on U.S. soil, it had lower distribution costs. Its tradition of gradual detail improvement saved the expense of frequent, radical retooling. And its spare, focused two-engine product line made it relatively economical for the company to respond quickly to the market.

These events had their results. By 1987 Harley's $3,995 Sportster competed with the Honda Shadow at $3,898. A new advertising campaign stressed Harley as the traditional, real, one-and-only American motorcycle and pointed out higher H-D resale value. Aggressive licensing and marketing of the Harley name and logo backed that up. Many riders came to realize that the Japanese copies were merely caricatures of the real thing. In the macho world of motorcycling, too much refinement was now a bad thing. In contrast to the sewing machine smoothness and sameness of the imports, only a Harley filled the rider with a sense of power. On a Harley, riders know when they shift gears. And the company began to maximize this former liability as a promotional asset.

It wasn't just pricing and PR that were changing at Harley, either. In 1984 they embarked on a major modernization of their Big Twin engines (and later the Sportster) with the new Evolution line. This computer-designed engine, quickly tagged the Blockhead by enthusiasts, brought Harley to world class in reliability, power, quality, and oil tightness. A growing variety of chassis choices included rubber mounting, innovative rear suspensions, seating positions, and chain or belt drivetrains. Even a factory version of the old "Springer" fork returned—replete with modern geometry, metallurgy, and damping. To keep things on the boil, H-D management took the company public in 1987, with a stock offering on the New York Stock Exchange. With fresh capital, reduced debt, and the resources to respond to the market quickly and convincingly, Harley was on a roll.

And then Harley took an unheard-of step. With profits now safely assured, they voluntarily requested that a tariff benefiting them be lifted. It was a master public relations stroke. President Ronald Reagan visited a revitalized York manufacturing plant and gave management and factory workers his highest accolades for their contribution to the comeback. Today Harley's revival has convinced the deepest of doubters. Even after their share of the U.S. heavyweight motorcycle market—over 50 percent—became the envy of the industry, Harley continued innovating with the industry's first application of electrostatic powder coating of parts in 1991 and o-ring sealed drive chains for '92. Rumor has it that the factory's next-year production is already completely sold out. Consortia of overseas buyers scour garages and shops nationwide for Harleys—in any condition. So striking is the rebirth that the story has been told in a book about corporate excellence by business journalist Peter Reid, *Well Made in America*.

Credit goes to many for this resurgence, not the least due to Harley management for their foresight and tenacity. But a special place should be accorded to the long-time and loyal cadre of dealers nationwide, for the face that Harley presents to most riders is that of their local agency. H-D dealers' constant support, even love, for the company over a rollercoaster ride of years is perhaps best exemplified in the words of Phil Peterson. He makes it well known that he wants his gravestone to read: "I hope that I have done as much for Harley as they have done for me." And honorable mention also must go to Willie G. Davidson, grandson of one of the founders. Vice President of styling and product design, he is widely acknowledged as the Guru who has brought innovation to Harley in a way that attracts new trade-up buyers without turning off traditional customers. Under his guidance, Harley now offers a rich selection of models to satisfy all customer style preferences in the best tradition— from continental touring to cafe racing to bar-hopping, plus H-D's own line of customized parts for owners who want even more.

Harley-Davidson's miraculous comeback and survival after what seemed inevitable corporate death is a truly historical American lesson on how to elevate a corporation to a level of excellence. The Harley "miracle" which contributes to its mystique is a bona fide success story: a sterling example of American culture initiated in probably the early fifties, although some claim it reverts to the company's inception.

Its depth and direction were formalized in the sixties and now it is a part of the American lifestyle, not just a counterculture.

In final analysis, it is impossible to neatly dissect the Harley mystique. It's part patriotic triumph over adversity. It's part a rich tradition that has, as often knowingly as not, catered to and celebrated the individual, the customizer in all of us. It reflects the unique, independent experience of American long-distance motorcycling that cuts across all walks of life. Like last century's Wild West cowboys who roamed the range on their hay-fed steeds, you feel the wind, smell the air, and somehow seem more alive when you're motorcycle-mounted, outside any protective cocoon. Perhaps it is best summed up by the late and inveterate biker Malcolm Forbes, Sr., who penned in his book *More Than I Dreamed*: "Motorcycles are like racehorses. You want to have the best bloodlines...and that means a Harley, if you can."

So well entrenched is Harley in American folklore and the American spirit that to many riders their Sportster or Big-Twin is a personal piece of the American Dream. To dedicated Harley owners and riders, Harley-Davidson is hardly a mere mystique but a profound reality, a magnificent obsession, a pleasant contagion.

Harley-Davidson is alive and well, the mystique so unique to Harley flourishing as it never did before.

Along with the mystique has come a proliferation of Harley memorabilia, so much, in fact, that a strong collectible market has developed of items that have become rarities and unusual commemorative pieces.

Because of its tremendous sales value, the Harley logo is in great demand by manufacturers of everyday and specialty items. Today you can buy Harley shoes, sneakers, socks, wallets, watches, shirts, T-shirts, beer, cigarettes, knives, underwear, scarves, headbands, vests, jackets, hats, boots, swimsuits, ties, knick-knacks; the list of items with the Harley logo is endless and overwhelming. A large number of the items have become sought-after collectibles, and this book will give an overview of coveted items beginning with the initial masterpieces, the Harley bikes themselves.

CHAPTER 2

HARLEY-DAVIDSON MOTORCYCLES— THE HISTORICAL COLLECTIBLES

Since the Harley-Davidson Motorcycle Company was primarily involved in the production of two-wheeled transportation, it is their motorcycles, particularly older vintage models that dominate the Harley collectible field.

There is an old adage: "Old Harleys never die, they just get rebuilt." This axiom is very true and there are a host of old Harleys around in various stages from mint (exceedingly rare), to refurbished, to all-out renovated and restored. Naturally, mint condition, unrestored pieces will have greater value, but in the realm of auto and motorcycle refurbishing, restoration does not necessarily lessen the value to a great extent. Following is a cross section of Harley-Davidson rare or collectible motorcycles produced since the company's inception.

THE FIRST "SINGLES"

Harley's initial model, produced in the diminutive manufacturing facility, a wooden shed, was made and assembled by hand. It is believed that only one motorcycle was produced in the starting year of 1903.

The simple bicycle type frame housed a single cylinder engine of about 25 cu. in. (400 c.c.), and the size of the flywheel was doubled. In 1906 a color scheme for the bike that soon got the nickname "Silent Gray Fellow" was developed in Renault gray and carmine striping. The "silent" aspect of the motorbike, the sound-damping exhaust mufflers.

By 1908 the fledgling motorbikes had their own identification systems. Since true production of the first models did not commence until 1904, the 1908 models were considered fifth-year models. The list price for the early Harleys: a mere $200. The first models, no bigger than a standard large bicycle, sported a 51-inch wheelbase and a frame height of 21½ inch, utilized 2¼ inch detachable tires, and featured a spring bicycle type seat.

The "Silent Gray Fellow," the earliest successful Harley-Davidson, is now a piece of Harley-Davidson as well as American history. © Copyright Harley-Davidson.

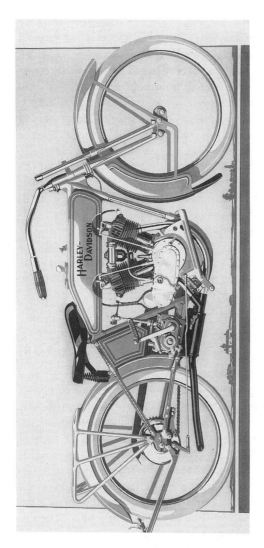

The first V-Twins were offered in 1909. This 1915 3-speed 61 cu. in. model featured inlet over exhaust.

© Copyright Harley-Davidson.

THE V-TWIN (1907–21)

The V-Twin engine concept, predecessor of all current Harley-Davidson engines, was first made available to the public in 1909. The "6-D" as the model was called contained a precision Bosch magneto and offered 26- or 28-inch wheel options. Again, the Renault gray finish was standard. In 1910, a "7-E" racing model was offered to only a few select customers. These unique early racers are virtually nonexistent and the rarest of the rare. In 1911 Harley patented an idler mechanism in which a lever and gear arrangement served as an ersatz clutch. With this setup the driver did not have to overcome motor-train drive in order to stop, just disengage the drive. Oil was gravity fed through a glass inspection tube that led directly to the crankcase. The oil feed system lubricated both fly-wheel and crank while directly feeding oil to the bearings. This added positive lubrication system was essential since the engine was now bored out to 61 cu. in., which necessitated more adequate lubri-cation for the 1912 models.

Early V-Twins are rare, exceedingly so, and if any surface, they are usually semi-emaciated. The few pristine collection pieces are like endangered species. A magnificent 1914 vintage 61 cu. in. Twin is exhibited in the Harley-Davidson York Museum.

Single Cylinder "5-35" (1913–18)

Another single was introduced in 1913, designated the 5-35, which stood for 5 horsepower 35 cu. in. It contained an iron cylinder and head and a specially heat-treated steel piston, a hollow steel wrist pin, and a connecting rod fashioned from a steel I-beam. This specific engine featured an all-alu-minum crankcase and the crank itself revolved in phosphor-bronze bushings. There were dual cam shafts involved, one for the inlet valves, one for the exhaust valves. The engine was fed by a Schebler carburetor and the ignition for this model was a Bosch high-tension magneto. A roller chain from the crank sprocket to the rear wheel hub sprocket served as the drive train. Clutch engagement was by a lever located on the left side of the vehicle. In an emergency situation caused by engine failure, the clutch could be disengaged and the motorbike ped-aled away.

The 5-35 models featured two-speed transmis-sions up to 1915, when Harley began using new H-

The Model IOE was introduced in 1914, a very rare piece and hard to find. © Copyright Harley-Davidson.

D three-speed units. These bikes were capable of speeds in excess of 60 mph. A 1913 Harley-Davidson single is currently on display at the Smithsonian Institution in Washington, D.C.

37 cu. in. Flat Twin (1919–22)

In 1919 a Sport Twin model, conceived in the last year of the First World War, was introduced featuring a newly designed motor, a front-to-rear opposed Twin configuration. The 37 cu. in. engine was mounted low in the frame. The machine was very fuel efficient, almost vibration free, and quiet. Its only drawback was that it was too slow in comparison to the competitive counterparts. The bike featured chain drive, a three-speed sliding gear transmission, and a Brewster green paint job with decorative gold striping. The Sport Twin was offered between 1919 and 1922. Not very popular on the road, the limited quantities and unique design make it a rare collectible fetching far more (if you can find one) than its original $340.

74 cu. in. Twin (1922–29)

Here we have the grandfather of the Big twin so popular today. In its era it was known as the Superpowered Twin and was first featured in the 22 J.D. with a $3\frac{7}{16}$ bore and a 4-inch stroke. Harley claimed that this new model was capable of producing 81 hp or better. Fuel economy was good, 40 to 60 miles on a gallon of gas. This heavy-duty model sported an efficient ignition and lighting system consisting of a 6-volt generator ignition unit, a storage battery, distributor, and hi-intensity spark coil. Alemite lubrication was also offered for all bearing surfaces, which could be applied by means of an Alemite container that forced grease into lubrication fittings by revolving the Alemite container handle.

Another major breakthrough was the use of aluminum for the new 74's pistons. By employing aluminum, with its superior heat dissipation qualities, the chance of piston seizure was reduced. The tank on the 74 began the early evolution to the tear drop style adopted for consecutive models. Initial cost of the 1922 "74" was $360.

21 CU. IN. SINGLE (1926-35)

Though not a popular Harley model, the 21 cu. in. Single was in production for ten years. It was a stoic little machine but more accepted by the Europeans and Australians than the American bike buffs of the era. This dependable motor scooter was made available in both side valve and overhead valve versions, the "Peashooter" doing quite well in AMA racing competition.

Four versions of the 21 cu. in. Single were marketed: a side valve magneto model, an overhead valve magneto model, a side valve generator model, and an overhead generator model. The overhead configurations were the more potent versions. Side valve models sported iron (alloy) pistons while the overhead models offered lighter weight aluminum racing pistons. The racing type engines featured special heads that squished vaporized fuel toward the plug for improved, more positive combustion. This 1926 Harley model is a rarity and a highly coveted collectible, worth much, much, much more than its initial selling price of $210 to $275.

HARLEY MODEL J, J.D. (1927–29)

The original design of the 1927 Harley J was based upon the Twin 61 cu. in. powerplant. Both engines shared the same frame, lighting, ignition system, and 22-amp battery.

Not many 61 cu. in. models surface in this country (they were built for the European market). They come with a ride-off stand in the front as well as in the rear, which was mandatory in Europe. The 61 cu. in. motor features a $3\frac{5}{16}$" bore coupled to a $3\frac{1}{2}$" stroke. The 74 cu. in. J.D. motor offered a

This 61 cu. in. 1927 Model J is particularly rare in that it is a European version featuring a front and rear kick stand. The bike is owned by Phil Peterson.

bore of $3^{7}/_{16}$" with a 4" stroke. Both engines contained lightweight iron alloy pistons, and the motors were lubricated by a specially designated mechanical pump supplemented by a hand pump. A foot operated clutch assisted in shifting and engaging the three-speed progressive sliding transmission. Very few of these machines exist today and most of them have been restored. Still, they retain very high collectible value.

45 CU. IN. V-TWIN (1929–51)

Another classic Harley and Harley engine is found in the 45 V-Twin. Harley went all-out in production on the 45's, issuing three variations on the 45 theme in 1929. There was a standard 45 DL model bike, a more potent high-compression 45 DLD model, and a low-compression model 45D to be utilized with an optional side hack. Alloy pistons were stock issue in all 45's from 1930 on. The high-compression model was phased out in 1932, but the remaining models remained standard issue and were designated "R" models, retaining their mechanical features up to 1936. After 1936, the 45's were designated "W" models and featured the recirculating oil system designed for the 1936 Knucklehead. The 45 engine was also the designated powerplant for the early Servi-Car motors, famous three-wheeled delivery trucks of the thirties.

The 45's have remained coveted classic collectibles despite their inherent sluggishness, weak transmissions, and tendency to leak oil. They are becoming scarce in good condition today, though a myriad of them were produced within their production span.

35.50 CU. IN. SINGLE (1929–36)

In 1929 Harley-Davidson took a step back to step forward in creating the 35.50 Single to appease racers. They crafted a new head design by taking half of a 61 cu. in. motor (the head), then grafting it to a

This rare, pristine 1942 "45" model belongs to Reynold Maragni of Brothers III and is for sale for $12,000.

Close-up of the "45" engine, a lot of which are still around and, though valued collectibles, are not as coveted as other or classic vintage Harleys.

1929 lower end. In 1929, the Model C engine, as it was known, was housed in a 21 cu. in. Harley frame, but in 1932 it was transferred to the 45 cu in. model. The "C" featured a three-speed progressive sliding gear transmission, H-D generator, waterproof coil, five plate storage battery, and relay cutout to automatically open and close the battery generator circuit. The bike was painted in olive green with a center gold stripe and maroon accent stripes.

74 CU. IN. VL (1930–40)

Faulty in its original design, the 74 VL had a bad engine, a bad clutch, and undersized flywheels. The frames broke, the exhausts clogged up. Nevertheless, Harley management touted the VL as "the greatest achievement in motorcycle history." Harley took matters into their own hands and, to their credit, resolved all the problems of the VL. In 1936 a VLD model was issued featuring side valves. Other innovations served to heighten interest in the newer V series machines: extra-heavy duplex primary chain, easily removable wheel, 27×4.00 balloon tires, a heavier, sturdier frame, improved 22-amp battery, waterproof coil, four full gallons of gasoline storage. The color scheme was also olive green embellished with vermilion striping. In 1932

In 1936, the 74 cu. in. OHV "Knucklehead" model was introduced and it became a popular street machine. A few "Knuckles" are still around but they command high dollars in original or restored conditions. They are coveted collectibles. © Copyright Harley-Davidson.

*The Knucklehead engine was a refined piece of engineering
for its time and old Knuckleheads are still reliable today.*
© Copyright Harley-Davidson.

an art deco design was added to the sides of the fuel
tanks. The selling price for the VL, VS, and VC
models of the 74 was around $350.

80 CU. IN. SIDE VALVE TWIN (1936–45)

The last of the side valve twins was the 80 cubic
incher introduced in 1936, which lasted the six
years preceding the revolutionary Knucklehead.
The side valve twins designated UL and ULH featured the proven Y manifold (intake) plus deep
finned heads for optimum cooling and the new
combustion chamber design so popular with the 74.
The new original four-speed transmission exhibited some shortcomings, but these were remedied
after the first year of production. The decision to
drop the 80 cu. in. UL models was due to a short-
age of materials after the Second World War and
the immense popularity and dominance of the revolutionary Knucklehead, which soon came upon
the scene.

The 1936 Harley-Davidson dashboard was uniquely styled.
© Copyright
Harley-Davidson.

THE "KNUCKLEHEAD" 61, 74 CU. IN. OVERHEAD VALVE MODELS

The Knucklehead originally was released as a 61 cu. in. model but gained wider acceptance and popularity as a 74 cu. in. OHV engine bike. Introduced in 1941, it overcame some initial lubrication problems manifest in the 61 cu. in. version. In response to public demand for increased cubes and higher power output, Harley decided to market a motorcycle with above average performance for solo riding, and adequate power to handle an added sidecar with ease.

The greatest mechanical improvement was a centrifugal oil pump that allowed equal and constant oil distribution to all parts of the engine. An r.p.m. regulated bypass valve shut at high speeds to allow maximum lubrication of the motor. At lower r.p.m.'s the value opened up to bypass the gear case and recycle up to the oil supply tank. In 1941, gear driven pumps were installed on all the 61 and 74 OHV engines.

A more efficient clutch was another boon in the 74 models. The clutch consisted of three steel discs, three fiber discs, and one spring disc, allowing seven friction contact areas. A friction surface

The 1941 FL 74 OHV, another rare "Knuckle-head" model. © Copyright Harley-Davidson.

increase of over 60 percent more than previous clutches guaranteed smoother, more positive shifting. Everything on the Knucklehead was either bigger or better. The 74 OHV model was produced in limited quantities during the Second World War due to material limitations. Even after the war in 1946 and 1947 production was limited. The Knuckleheads are considered Harley classics and have escalated in value over the years. They have become quite scarce and only occasionally does one find a pristine original or exacting restoration. You would pay less for a brand-new updated Harley than for an A-1 condition Knucklehead.

MODEL S-125 (1947–52)

This is an intriguing collectible in that it is the only Harley two-stroke (two-cycle) engine motorcycle. It was based on a pre-World War II design by German DKW engineers who forfeited the patent rights when Germany lost the war. B.S.A. (Birmingham Small Arms) in England and Harley-Davidson took up the design. The bike was lightweight and 10,000 were put into production and in Harley showrooms throughout the country. But traditional Harley riders couldn't endear themselves to the two-cycle lightweight Harley. The bike is both a Harley and not a Harley. It's an oddball. The lightweight is a one-cylinder machine displacing 7.6 cu. in.

MODEL K 45, 55 CU. IN.
V-TWIN (1952–56)

The 1952 Model K is another Harley-Davidson classic motorcycle and a predecessor to the Sportsters released in 1957. The K resembles motorcycles as we visualize them today, with the transmission incorporated into the crankcase. In 1952 the all-in-one motor was a first for the company which was used to designing motorcycles with separate motors and transmissions within the frame.

The model K's motor was a 45 cu. in. twin cylinder side valve unit, four stroke, air cooled, featuring aluminum alloy cylinder heads and enclosed valve gear. The engine featured a $2\frac{1}{4}$" bore and a $3\frac{13}{16}$" stroke.

The transmission integrated into the crankcase was a four-speed type with larger gears for extra durability. The clutch is hand released, foot shifted; the clutch unit itself is a multiple dry disc unit with bonded fiber clutch facings.

The rear suspension is comprised of a swing arm attached to two hydraulic shock absorbers with swingarm pivot points featuring preloaded Timkin bearings. The Model K's were available in Persian red, Rio blue or gloss black. Frames were all black. The Model K is a rare and valued collectible. A special KH model was issued in 1953 which featured hotter cams, less chrome, and flatter handlebars.

The K model Harley's are coveted collectibles and classic vintage motorcycles. The "King," Elvis Presley, owned and rode a KH and his bike is the most famous Harley collectible, currently on display at the Harley-Davidson museum.

Elvis originally purchased the 1956 KH from a Memphis Harley dealer, making the standard $50 a month payment. He rode the bike often in the wee hours of the night with one of his cronies, Fleming Horne. Horne loved riding and he loved Elvis's pepper-red and white KH.

One day Elvis bestowed the bike on Horne along with the commitment to continue the payments. Horne kept and maintained the bike and a few years ago rejected an offer of $250,000 for it from a Japanese investor. Horne felt the bike should be kept in the States. Harley-Davidson agreed and made Horne an offer he couldn't refuse, which was never disclosed.

There is also a 1966 FL-based Chopper that Elvis once owned but rarely rode as he didn't like the way choppers handled or the sixties image they projected.

Elvis's KH is probably the highest valued H-D collectible, simply because it belonged to an American icon.

Sportster XL (1957–87)

Ten cubic inches larger than its design predecessor, the "K," the Sportster XL was a marketing sensation and one of the best-selling Harley models of the sixties. The motor, an integrated unit with no separately housed transmission, boasted 83.9 cu. in. This 883 c.c. motor produced 40 horsepower at 5,500 rpm and, with a 7.5 to 1 compression ratio, was the muscle bike of its time. Rear suspension was by means of automotive type shock absorbers.

Two years later the XLCH hit the streets, an upgraded Sportster with higher compression domed pistons, larger intake and exhaust valves, and aluminum tappets. In 1959 the XL and XLCH boosted horsepower by means of a hi-lift intake cam and reworked exhaust cams. The Sportster tank became a chopper innovation and many choppers of the sixties era, Harley and otherwise, relied on Sportster tanks as specialty extras.

In 1968 the Sportster lost its kick starter and the electrics were upgraded to a 12-volt system also incorporating an electric starter. Spin-offs of the XLCH, the XLCR, and the XL-750, strictly performance machines, penetrated the performance bike market.

In the late seventies fewer than 3,400 XLCR cafe racers were produced, making them limited in number, hence rating very high on the collectible market in pristine, out-of-the-factory condition. Willie G. Davidson, Harley vice president and descendant of the original Davidson who formed the company, owns one, and one is exhibited at the Rodney Gott Museum in York, PA.

In 1986, the XCH Sportster received the new V2 Evolution 883 c.c. engine which featured the new "Blockhead" design, hydraulic lifters, and a totally redesigned top end.

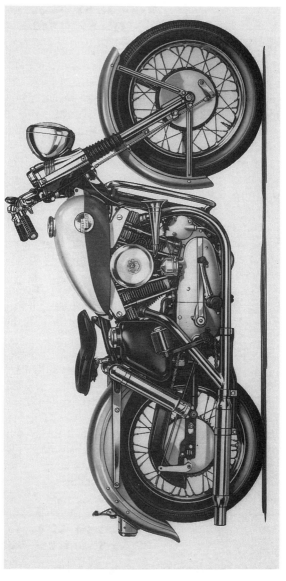

The very classic 1957 Sportster design XL. Always sought after and coveted collectibles. © Copyright Harley-Davidson.

PANHEAD 61, 74 CU. IN.
MODELS (1948–65)

The Panhead motor, furthering the evolution of the Big Twin, came upon the scene as early as 1948, when it emerged in a Hardtail frame. It was featured on the 1958 Duo-Glide and as late as 1965 on the Electra-Glide, giving it a lifespan of eighteen years. The new motor of 1948 featured aluminum cylinder heads, which dissipated heat quickly, plus push rod hydraulic lifters in the valve train. The new lifters inhibited tappet noise, while oil flow and pressure were also upgraded. An improved oil pump transferred 25 percent more oil to the top end of the motor, and all the oil passages were internal. The new improved Panhead 74 weighed about eight pounds less than the Knucklehead, but served up as much power.

The year after they were released, the Panhead-powered Harleys got a new and welcome addition: hydraulic front forks to improve the ride and the bikes' handling.

In 1950 and 1951, the Panhead got a 10-horsepower boost, and in 1952 the first foot shift Panhead was introduced.

The 1958 to 1964 Duo-Glides are still encountered on the highways; many still exist. The late Panheads are not as coveted collectibles as the early or initial offerings in either stock or restored condition. Early footshift 1952 models are sought after and 1948 FL Harleys are rare collectibles.

SHOVELHEAD 74, 80 CU. IN.
V-TWIN (1966–86)

In 1966 the Shovelheads made their debut, in the FL models (54 hp) with the chassis coupled to a modified X-series front fork. The FLs and FLHs were initially offered in optional red, white, and blue decor, a new improved head design, and a Tillotson diaphragm carburetor. The only shortcoming of the earlier models were inadequate

The first year of the Panhead was 1948, hence these models are sought after and valuable in stock, pristine condition. This model, owned by Reynold Maragni, had a showroom price tag of $23,000, more than some current Harley-Davidson offerings.

A later Panhead
version, the 1949
Hydra-Glide, also
a sought after col-
lector's item. ©
Copyright Harley-
Davidson.

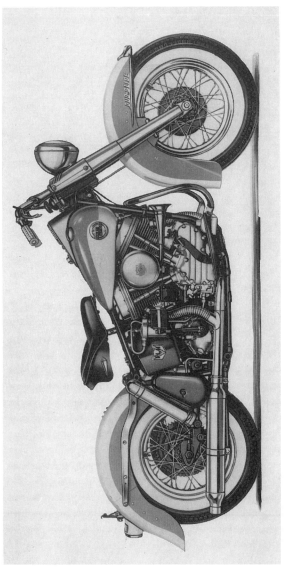

Another collector special, the 1958 74 cu. in. FLH Duo-Glide. This was the earliest model to feature hydraulic front and rear suspension. © Copyright Harley-Davidson.

Close-up of Maragni's machine shows that it is in pristine condition, well worth the asking price.

brakes and the tendency for the engines to leak oil, problems which were easily remedied.

In 1971, the Super-Glide hit the market with another Willie G. Davidson design that made it the aesthetic epitome of cruising bike designs and a styling concept that affected later Harley and even Japanese cruiser designs. Designated the FX, the Super Glide was the first motorcycle model to be considered a factory custom, so-to-speak. The design was a keen and workable grafting of the Super Glide frame with Sportster-like front forks, creating a total new look.

Operationally, it was sound. It would kick-start easily; the transmission was strong, smooth, and reliable, while it was seventy pounds lighter than its predecessor. In 1973, disc brakes became standard issue, and the FXE was introduced in 1974 featuring electric starting. In 1980 the FLTs hit the road with hotter sparking due to V-Fire pointless ignition systems.

Following the Shovelheads, Harley redesigned their motorcycles to introduce the new Evolution engines and Softail chassis. The Evolutions are the currently coveted riding machines, but too new to be classed as collectibles.

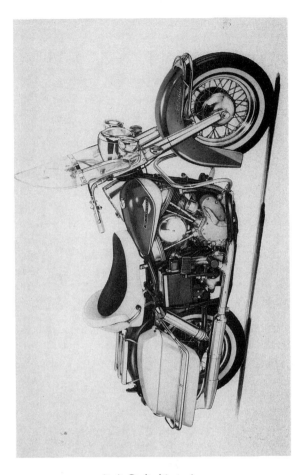

Another rare Panhead model, the famed 1960 Electra-Glide. It was considered the finest riding machine of its era.
© Copyright Harley-Davidson.

*The Shovelhead engine was the next engineering milestone
following the Panhead. Engines in pristine condition are
collected, even out of motorcycles.*

*The first Evolution Sportster engine introduced in the early
1980's is today a mainstay in Sportster models offered
in a standard and high-performance model.*

The revolutionary Evolution engine, known as the
"Blockhead," is an engineering masterpiece and has been used
in Big Twin motorcycles from 1984 to the present.

© Copyright Harley-Davidson.

HARLEY-DAVIDSON COLLECTIBLE MEMORABILIA

Someday, someone will have to do an Encyclopedia of Harley collectibles; that's what it would take to categorize the voluminous ranks of Harley memorabilia. The list is endless since Harley-Davidson retains the unique distinction of having its highly regarded logo on virtually anything you can imagine: shirts, Levi's, boots, belts, underwear (male and female), socks, sneakers, jackets, hats, scarves, headbands, earrings, necklaces, belt buckles, hats (all kinds), wallets, kitchenware, knives, conchos, key chains, can openers, beer, cigarettes, ladies lingerie, swimsuits, T-shirts, vests (leather and denim), hundreds of patches, bumper stickers, license plates, tableware, glassware, bracelets, buttons, telephones, radios, plastic models, Franklin Mint Commemorative Bike issues, playing cards, collecting cards....GEEZ!, one could go on forever.

Aside from memorabilia and old trivia, Harley also sanctions a number of collectible items that are manufactured specifically as collectible items in a current era that abounds in the manufacture of collectible items.

A book of this nature cannot run the whole gamut of Harley items, collectible and otherwise. We will, however, endeavor to put you onto some pieces worthy of merit which will assist you in defining or accumulating your own personalized Harley-Davidson collection. The avenues can be wide and far reaching. Some of the examples we present may surprise and astound you. You may see some items that are totally new or alien to you. As I stated before, the prospects are virtually unlimited and certainly far-reaching in both scope and nature.

CAR COLLECTIBLES

Every so often Harley will issue a commemorative truck or vehicle, and these are predestined to become collectibles. A recent addition to this roster is a limited edition reproduction of a 1936 Dodge truck in 1:25 scale. The red and black oil truck in baked enamel is resplendent in Harley signage and logos. The truck's current value is $40 but will soon accelerate in value.

A special issue 1940 Ford truck bank, also of die cast metal, limited in production (1:25 scale), allows dealership imprint on top. The reproductions are going for $42 and rate as collectible items.

Bike model buffs will love the new Police Servi-Car in 1:12 scale with a steerable front end. The Servi-Car box opens to present a coin slot, handcuffs, and baton. Limited edition at $64.

KNIVES

A host of knives have been marketed by Harley-Davidson, some as special issue and many as commemorative items. All types and configurations are produced, from small pocket knives to buck knives and hunting knives. Many feature fine hand or machine engraving. There is a special series of ten collector's knives, two available and eight more to be released in the near future. The current and second offering is the Buy Back Mini Knife II. This mini-knife commemorates the original full-size "Buy Back" knife issued prior to 1981. The Mini Knife II is available at $105.

The first ten collector's knives, issued in 1983, are rare and have doubled and tripled in value. The mini-knife series is a duplication but still are very collectible. A miniature of the original Harley eighty-fifth anniversary knife, made of high carbon steel, is engraved with a wood handle and brass bolsters, and can be currently obtained for $125.

COINS

Harley also has its own specialized mint. A series of five collector coins depicting engines on one side and the Harley-Davidson bar and shield on the flip side are also in production. The fourth in a series of five is now available in a black velvet box. The coins contain one Troy ounce of silver and are about $1\frac{1}{2}$ inches in diameter. Each coin is $38.

PUBLICATIONS (PROMOTIONAL)

The most notable of Harley-Davidson publications, which are rare, are copies of Harley's own magazine published years ago, *The Enthusiast*. This magazine was devoted to the motorcycle sport with a total Harley slant. Usually the covers featured name stars of the entertainment field. Roy Rogers on his Harley grace the cover of one issue. In September of 1942, *The Enthusiast* featured Clark Gable on his full Harley-Davidson dresser while the centerfold of the same issue featured Gene Autry with his "iron horse." Copies of *The Enthusiast* from 1940 to 1950 fetch between $20 and $50 each.

In the fifties, Elvis Presley was featured on his Sportster KH model which is now a museum piece and probably one of the most highly valued of Harley collectibles. The Presley *Enthusiast* issue has

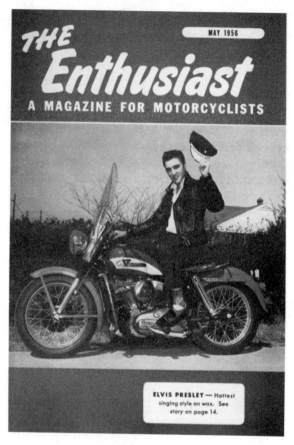

MAY 1956

THE Enthusiast

A MAGAZINE FOR MOTORCYCLISTS

ELVIS PRESLEY — Hottest
singing style on wax. See
story on page 14.

In May 1956, The Enthusiast *featured Elvis Presley on its
cover. He is shown here on his KH which is now owned by
Harley-Davidson and is a popular item in its museum.*

been bought by collectors for up to $75 in pristine
condition.

Sales literature and catalogs also rate high as collectible rarities. Catalogs from the early Harley-
Davidson years are extremely valuable and coveted
by literature collectors. Issues such as the 1915,
1916, and 1917 catalogs, for example, will attain
collectible sale prices between $100 and $500. The
rare 1919 World War I catalog is also worth up to
$500 in mint condition.

Catalogs issued in the twenties will bring from $50 to $200 in the collectible mart. Catalogs issued in the thirties go from $50 up to $150. In the ten years spanning 1930 to 1940, there were some price fluctuations according to the artistic quality of the catalog design. The beautiful 1931 catalog is dazzling four-color and rates as high as $300 in tip-top shape.

For the forties issues, top-end values decline, though the bottom end for not-so-cherry copies remains at $50. Pristine issues within this time span easily get $150. In the last third of the forties era, brochures and catalogs span the $25 to $100 price range. It seems that within each consecutive ten-year period the catalog values decline about a third from the previous ten-year period.

CIGARETTES

In the 1980's, Harley Davidson entered the realm of cigarettes, and various designs from early cigarette package conceptions to date have graced special issue Harley cigarette packs. Early issues are not rare, but are interesting collectibles at $2 to $8 per pack. It is alleged that Harley-Davidson wishes to dissolve the Harley-cigarette association and if this comes about, older as well as contemporary cigarette packs are sure to escalate in value.

ADVERTISING MEMORABILIA

This encompasses everything from brochures and magazine ads to posters, far too many to enumerate or evaluate.

Some items here are worthy of mention for their rarity and value. The very rare Harley-Davidson Hillclimber poster from way back in 1928 is valued between $3,000 and $12,000. That's more than some older and some current motorcycles attain in value.

Schabers Motorcycle Shop calendars (Ithaca, N.Y.) from 1932 to 1938, are priced from $100 to $350.

SIGNAGE

Signage is highly collectible material, and is even regarded so by antique dealers, and Harley-Davidson has certainly made a formidable contribution to vintage signage.

One rare form of signage dating back to the 1930's was a Harley-Davidson Motorcycle Shop valance for placement in shop windows. It was a decal-type sign featuring the Harley-Davidson bar and shield and is today valued at $200.

In the 1930's, Harley stores featured a prominent neon sign, which was usually hung over the sales counter. This very rare sign is a coveted sign collectible valued between $2,000 and $4,000.

In the thirties and forties, tin signs were also featured in shops, windows or on building facades. A rare rectangular sign first issued in 1930 was orange and black on a white background which featured the Harley-Davidson bar and shield logo, also reading from left to right on top: MOTORCYCLES, SERVI-CARS. In the lower lefthand corner was PARTS; the lower right: SERVICE. This relic is today worth between $400 and $900.

A squarish sign of the forties, which also featured a bar and shield, designated the shop as an authorized dealer and had the shop name embossed and painted on the face. Under the shop name were

Signs of this type were seen in the 1950's, though their origin can be traced to the 1940's. They are rare collectibles and hard to find today. They go for $1,000 and up.

*This flat metal sign was provided to dealers in the mid-1930's
and was used as late as the 1950's.*

*This sign was issued to promote the Hydra-Glide.
These metal signs could be found in Harley dealerships in
1949 and the early 1950's.*

the words in bold caps: SALES and SERVICE. This
sign, typical of the dealership signs of the forties,
will fetch from $100 to $400.

In the late fifties and sixties, Harley went to
light-up signs. A rectangular, molded plastic sign,
with a yellow background sporting the bar and
shield in black trim, goes today for $200 to $650.
Another lighted sign, circa the same period, was
used by franchised dealers. It was a long rectangular
sign featuring the Harley-Davidson logo on a yel-

This sign was circa 1930 to 1940.

They don't have to be Harley issue to be Harley collectibles. Here's a Nike-Reebok promo, sure to be a collector piece.

low backdrop. This sign today is valued at between $200 and $500.

Another rare piece not found in quantity was a Harley-Davidson Gas Pump seen around the fifties and sixties, though not in abundance. The pump illustrated here is owned by Sonny Steel and sits in the U.S. Steel showroom in Fort Lauderdale, Florida, as an eye-catching conversation piece that attracts a lot of attention. The pump was purchased by Steel for $4,000 in mint condition.

Sonny Steel owns this rare showpiece featured in his U.S. Steel, Ft. Lauderdale, showroom. It's a 1950's era gas pump and was purchased by Steel for $3,000.

TRADING CARDS

Trading cards go back to the early part of the twentieth century, when they became sales incentives for chewing gum. Baseball and sports cards were the initial offerings and in later years, collectors began to realize the value of cards as collector's items.

About five years ago, some savvy entrepreneurs got together and began issuing special commemorative sets of Harley-Davidson Motorcycle cards. These became an instant success not only with kids but also with Harley-Davidson aficionados who flocked to Harley dealers to buy the boxed sets. The beautiful renderings originally came in three individually boxed sets and sold initially for about $35. They were soon fetching $50 for each boxed set. Today, if you can find the original sets, they will fetch from $75 to $100 in mint, unopened condition. Opened sets themselves will fetch well over $50 in pristine condition.

Harley collector cards are accelerating in value. They sold for about $50 a set, and now fetch over $100 in unopened mint state.

CLOTHING

Past and present, the quantity of Harley-Davidson clothing is astounding. Old clothing is rare and limited, highly rated in collectible circles, exceedingly hard to come by. The last decade is responsible for a proliferation of garments, boots and other fashion sundries. The value of current pieces, particularly items manufactured by and distributed by Harley-Davidson, will accelerate as the articles are discontinued and replaced by newer ones, which in turn will have extra value in the future.

By far, the most valuable of the clothes collectibles are items dating back to the thirties, when Harley-Davidson began marketing riding gear for sale through their distributors and dealerships. Clothes as accessory items were an astute marketing gimmick and it was found that some dealers could accrue more revenue on apparel than on service and repairs.

First choice for riding gear is leather for its scrape resistance and durability. Black leather jackets, brown bomber jackets, leather pants, and good boots comprise the typical sound riding gear of the past and present.

In the thirties, Harley-Davidson circulated a host of riding sweaters in varied colors. The sweaters were long sleeved with a winged Harley patch on the front. They were zippered halfway up so that they could be worn shirt-collar style or zippered-up turtleneck style to protect against the elements. Another style, and one favored by lady riders, was a v-neck long-sleeved sweater also emblazoned with a Harley wing insignia on the front. The standard and v-neck versions today are worth between $200 and $600 on the collectible market.

In the late thirties and through the forties, Harley-Davidson popularized their racing and riding jerseys. Again, they were pull-over type, zippered type offerings similar to the riding shirts of the thirties. The name HARLEY-DAVIDSON in large, bold black uppercase type predominated on the front face of the shirt. The famous Harley jerseys are valued between $200 and $600.

Jackets:

Leather jackets are the staple of riding. There are a host of generic leather jackets, some going back to the early days of motorcycling. The oldies are rarities, but the more standard type is the archetypical motorcycle jacket prevailing in the fifties, made famous by Marlon Brando in the movie *The Wild One*. This style fits the stereotype for badass bikers, but conventional riders also opt to own them for their looks, comfort, great styling cut, and general riding safety. The *Wild One* jacket has come down through the years and there are so many of them out on the market that their value is seldom over store value.

From the fifties onward, Harley-Davidson did promote lines of riding jackets, leather and otherwise, as part of their aftermarket sales program. Some older Harley riding jackets are worthy of note and considered collectible items.

A Harley-Davidson black riding jacket and pants outfit with a 50th Anniversary, Sturgis, South Dakota, patch was a special issue circa the 1960's. The set, which originally retailed for about $60, today brings between $100 and $300. A special brown riding jacket and pants set of the fifties era fetches between $200 and $500.

In the early seventies, under new ownership of AMF, a special cloth riding jacket was marketed featuring new tailored styling. The jacket displays the AMF-Harley-Davidson name inside and under the collar, button-down breast pockets, button-down front and long sleeves, and buttoned cuffs and slash belly pockets. This fine-looking collectible riding jacket is worth about $150 today in pristine shape.

Footwear

Footwear items as Harley collectibles are iffy....Most riding bootwear is made by old and new shoe manufacturers exclusively. Harley-Davidson does promote a line of leather footwear distributed and marketed under their auspices, at this point exhibiting mainly contemporary market value. Then, too, sneakers, etc., are also sold today on a wide scale. Whether these offerings will attain collectible value remains to be seen, though I predict some, on obsolescence, will rise in value.

In the thirties and forties, Harley-Davidson marketed police-style riding boots which today are collectible pieces. The boots are knee-rise types with top side buckles and straps and a strap over each instep. They are identifiable by a Harley-Davidson insignia imprinted on the soles. In mint condition a pair of these boots will go for $300.

Headgear

Headgear has varied from the early years to the present. The standard headgear of the past is totally different from the headgear of today, primarily because wearing a helmet when riding is becoming increasingly mandatory. Virtually all states now rules that helmets must be worn by the rider at all times while the vehicle is in motion. This also applies to the passenger.

In the old days way up into the fifties, Cop Style riding hats, as they were called, were a part of the bikeriders attire. Other popular headwear types were the leather bombardier or pilot caps. Winter fur hats, also worn by law enforcement officers, were also the vogue, complete with fold-down ear flaps.

Harley-Davidson promoted the aforementioned heavily, going so far as to provide point-of-sale posters to their dealers from 1949 on that heralded, "You'll look still better in a new Harley-Davidson cap." These caps were big sellers amongst Harley-

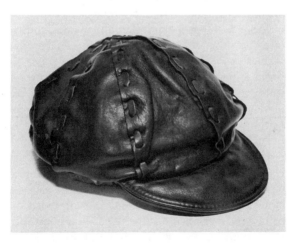

Older headgear is the rarest, but this "Willie G." leather cap is destined to be a valuable collectible in the future.

Davidson riding enthusiasts. A black and gold trimmed riding cap with Harley wings and logo and gold brocade was marketed around 1950 and these pieces today are worth between $75 and $100.

Throughout the forties and fifties, Harley-Davidson produced and marketed a host of Cop Style hats in a multitude of colors with varied brim trim. These vintage caps are worth from $75 to $150.

While scouting headgear pieces, don't overlook a 1930 to 1940 design motorcycle goggle, which is a coveted collectible. If you can pick up a pair in the original box, the value is highest. These goggles go for between $100 and $350.

In the fifties, corduroy brimmed caps were also marketed in various colors with a fold-up Harley wing emblem. These caps today are valued between $75 and $150.

T-Shirts

Multitudes! Multitudes! That's what my brain screams out when I think of the myriad of Harley-Davidson T-shirts produced in the last two decades alone. One can amass a large collection of Harley-Davidson T-shirts alone. Enough to fill all the wall space, all the drawers, all the bookshelves, and all the closets of a standard one-family house.

Early T-shirts, the more simplified ones, constitute the rarities in this realm. As types and art themes become obsolete, the values accelerate. T-shirts of defunct Harley dealerships, the names of which have faded into history, are top collectibles. Harley-Davidson commemorative and anniversary editions also hold higher value.

Around 1993, Harley-Davidson refused to sanction the use of their logo on aftermarket non-Harley dealer outlets. T-shirts printed with Harley or Harley-Davidson together with the name of a non-Harley establishment were also forbidden on pain of copyright infringement litigation. Any nonauthorized T-shirt containing HOG or dealer name with the same letters were ordered to cease using the three letter idiom. T-shirts from such

T-shirts are all over; some special Harley designs or commemorative issues will be collectible. The market is so saturated that standard T-shirts will have the least value. Limited run editions are favored for better collector value.

shops as Hog Heaven, Hog Hollow, and a host of other shops are rare items, and, though not true Harley collectible shirts, are ersatz collectibles which are popular with motorcycle paraphernalia collectors.

Commemorative Daytona, Sturgis, Laconia, and now Daytona Biktoberfest Harley sanctioned T-shirts are collector's items that increase in value each year after issue. Consecutive T-shirt collections are even rarer. T-shirt values are somewhat flexible but due to escalate depending on type and production runs. Older T-shirts can bring prices up to $150. More detailed studies must be made, however, and T-shirts must be cataloged in more detail before more exact values can be established. I would venture to say ball park figures on Harley collectible T-shirts are between $25 and $150, though most fit into the low-end bracket. One must also consider that thousands of T-shirts with a single design are printed and sold. Such heavy market saturation keeps the values stable.

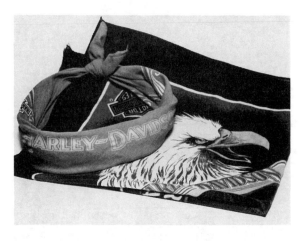

*Scarves and bandannas in old and limited issue deserve some
collector consideration. Here again high saturation
and production can limit value.*

Scarves - Bandannas

Here again we have a proliferation of items. There
is an incredible array, well into the hundreds. They
are an apparel staple and I don't know of a Harley
owner or buff who doesn't have one. Values are
minimal and there is no way of gauging their worth
as they are produced in such large quantities. Commemorative scarves will be of higher value.

BANNERS

In the old days Harley put out a series of banners
similar to college pennants. If you can locate the
old 1914-19 pennant, yellow with a twin cylinder
oldie and Harley-Davidson in red, you can acquire
a banner valued between $300 and $700.

A 1920 navy and white pennant will fetch $200
to $400. A gray one with red lettering of the same
vintage is valued at between $200 and $500. Similar
pennants of the forties and fifties go for between
$75 and $200.

Playing cards. Early sets have some value but are not high on the collectible list.

PLAYING CARDS

Many bikers are card players by nature, so naturally we must have Harley issue playing cards. Older decks will bring in $10 to $20 for a set, unopened, in mint condition.

BEER

"Bikers and suds, Miller or Bud." Beer is the unofficial champagne of the biker set. Old Harley cans and six-packs are worth $50 and up and commemorative ones such as the Daytona series even more.

A Daytona 1993 six-pack.

*Here's a special consecutive year set of beer cans
from 1986-94 owned by Sonny Steel. A great Daytona
collectible piece that could range in value from $100 to $300.
Not many of these around.*

Occasionally you will come upon special commemorative offerings in special displays and the collector display always nets a higher price.

PHONES

A few years back, Harley got into telephone communications, offering beautiful phones in the form of motorcycles. In time newer models will push the initial issue phones into the collectible bracket, but now one can pick one up for possible future investment.

*Harley phones are too numerous and common to be of any
value today. Tomorrow, they may be a prime collectible.*

Harley radios. They are all over. No value today but tomor-row, as each model is discontinued, they will become collectible.

RADIOS

Today Harley is heavy into radios and they are appealingly designed. Radios to fit your bike, radios to fit your home decor, and even radios to fit your pocket. A good assortment of radios have been licensed by Harley and, though not collectibles *per se* today, with planned model changes through the years, the Harley-Davidson radio of today is destined to be a collectible of tomorrow.

Another Harley-sanctioned radio. This will be of some collectible value in the future.

Believe it or not some folks collect Harley tanks, specifically the first year of model issue. They are valued by age, the earlier versions quadrupling in price, with fifties to sixties types only doubling in value (tripling if the tank is a limited edition model). Some folks just like to insert or screw on emblems. Unless from a pre-1940 era, these emblems have marginal value and are hardly ever found in pristine condition.

Some entrepreneurs collect tanks, exhibiting them as shown here. This is a late 1986 Softail Fatbob, which will accrue value down the road.

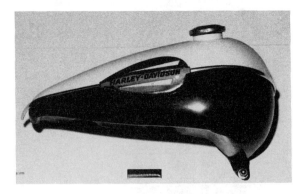

This tank goes back to the "Knucklehead" days. This tank goes back to the 1940's.

Some folks just like collecting tank plates and shields. Lesser value here, but nonetheless collectible.

Cushions like this can be bought at T.J. Maxx and K-Mart outlets. Collector value will increase in the far future.

PILLOWS

You can come across these at T.J. Maxx and similar outlets at decent prices. Not worth more than market value today, they may go up in price in the future, though at this point they are mainly reproductions.

WATCHES

There are a bunch of them; the rarest are the commemorative pieces. They will accelerate in collector values in years to come. Especially collectible

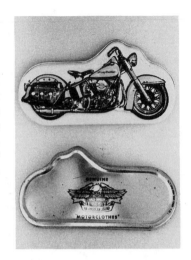

*Watches.
They are collectible,
but more so in
their special issue
cases such as these.
A good collector
investment.*

are the cases they come in and if you have the watch
and the box, investment values may be reached at a
later date.

TABLEWARE

In 1990 Harley-Davidson copyrighted a number of
tableware accessories which have found their way
into the Harley housewife's kitchen. They are

*This creamer was offered by Harley and dealers in 1990.
A new novelty piece, it will be a collectible
and is already sought after.*

*To check the authenticity of unusual Harley-Davidson
collectibles, check for the Harley copyright on the piece.*

Another great collector item: a Harley tank sugar bowl.

unique pieces and are easily identified as authentic
Harley collectibles by the H-D copyright insignia
on the bottom of the pieces. Part of the Harley
licensed line, these are unique pieces and should be
favored items on a collectible list. A wide assortment of beer glasses, drinking glasses, whiskey
glasses, cups, mugs, etc., are also marketed under
the auspices of Harley-Davidson.

Pins, buttons, buckles are all possible collectibles as newer ones are issued. Older pins of the 1930's, 1940's, and 1950's are the most collectible items.

PINS, EMBLEMS, AND BADGES

These number in the thousands: all styles, all sizes, and all types. Belt buckles also drastically expand this segment of add-on regalia worn by all types of bikers. They are all too numerous to be rare at this point (the current issue, that is).

Harley issued a number of special watch fobs in the years between 1915 and 1920 and these are rare and valued collectibles. In good condition, these fobs with distinctive Harley-Davidson logos are worth between $200 and $350 each. Fobs of the fifties era will fetch from $50 to $100, while newer fobs circa 1960 to 1970 bring from $50 to $100.

Early Harley-Davidson winged pins of the 1930's are rare and hard to find. These early pins are valued between $50 and $150. Old patches from the 1930's can fetch between $50 and $100.

Harley pins issued in the period between 1920 and 1980 will go for prices between $50 and $150.

OIL CANS

Oil cans sporting the Harley logo are also choice collectibles. If you can find a mint H-D oil can of the 1940's, it will be worth up to $150. A quart can of racing oil of the same era is valued at $200 in A-1 condition. A 1960 racing motor oil will bring $75 in tip-top condition. A 1950 Harley "Gunk" can is worth $80 in prime shape. If you are lucky enough to locate a one gallon can of Harley "genuine" motor oil first issued in 1930, it's worth from $300 to $700—a prime item; very few exist, hence the high dollar value. In the 1940's, Harley was packaging some of their oil in jars, which are worth between $50 and $200.

SCALE REPLICA MODELS

The Franklin Mint is widely known as a collectible house concentrating solely on collector items that are periodically manufactured on a limited basis.

Recently, Harley-Davidson authorized The Franklin Mint to create a series of replicas; highly detailed with movable parts and exquisite paintwork.

The 1957 Sportster model is a 1:10 scale die cast rendering of the first classic Harley superbike. The overhead-valve XL engine is infinitely detailed as is the rest of this 8½"-long model. The XL is detailed to the max, with chrome spoked wheels and chrome parts, and the headlight is surface-etched with authentic-looking grid lines. Over 130 separate parts have gone into the assembly of this accurate to-scale rendition of the ever popular Sportster.

To commemorate ninety years of the motorcycle police vehicle, which was introduced in 1907, Franklin Mint recreated the Harley-Davidson Electra-Glide Police Patrol bike, fully equipped

The Police Special issued by The Franklin Mint.
Photo courtesy of The Franklin Mint.

with a splendid array of operating features as found on the police prototypes. This handsome rendering is a full 9½" long. The bike is painted an impressive black and white and decked out in police bike regalia. In addition to a functional steering and suspension system, the scale model also offers storage bins that open from the top. The engine is an exact scaled-down rendering of the Shovelhead 1200 c.c. engine that was featured on the many Harley FLH model bikes. The shifting lever pivots and the brake pedals move. The tank-mounted console is also fully detailed, and a police helmet, handcuffs, and first-aid kit in miniature are provided as added accessories with the model. This replica, hand-assembled, is composed of more than 100 separate pieces. This model has been issued as a tribute to all law enforcement officers who rode Harley-Davidson bikes in the line of duty.

Harley buffs consider the Electra-Glide to be the ultimate touring machine. The Franklin Mint

*The Franklin Mint Electra-Glide highly detailed die-cast
replica of Harley-Davidson's ultimate touring machine.*
Photo courtesy of The Franklin Mint.

*Replica of the Great American Freedom Machine, the
Harley-Davidson Heritage Softail classic.*
Photo courtesy of The Franklin Mint.

Electra-Glide model is beautiful, highly detailed
scale model, $9\frac{1}{2}$" in length, in black paint with a
host of chrome parts, as in the full-sized touring
model. The model's suspension system, both front
and rear, works at the slightest touch. The V-Twin
Shovelhead engine is amazingly detailed. This road
model features a half fairing and a tour pack
mounted behind the seats that actually opens.

A fourth offering is Franklin Mint's recreation

Replica of the 1957 first Harley-Davidson Sportster XL.
Photo courtesy of The Franklin Mint.

of the Heritage Softail Classic, Harley's great American Freedom Machine. Like the other replicas, this one is also 9 ½" long and sports a two-tone paint job (ruby and beige). Shift and brake lines actually move and the bike is an example of fine superdetailing, assembled from 110 separate pieces. The handlebars turn the front wheel; the suspension system works and reacts as on the full-size version of the Harley classic.

The newest addition to the model line is the Harley "Biker Blues" bike. The original showbike was developed by Harley in conjunction with a sales promotion for the firm's specialty denim clothing line. The cycle is a custom version of the "Fat Boy" with an emulated "blue jean" paint job and rivets to give the unmistakable look of actual denim. A definite collector piece.

These five Harley-Davidson scale models are currently available from The Franklin Mint or their stores around the country. The retail price is $135 apiece but when the limited runs are depleted, the values will escalate in earnest. All the aforementioned models are approved and sanctioned by Harley-Davidson.

Though not as exacting or detailed as The Franklin Mint replicas, Matchbox, the miniature

*Two of the Matchbox Harley-Davidson series
with Shovelhead engines.*

*The Matchbox customizing showroom in which the building is
also the box to store the collectible piece.*

collectible car people released a few Harley-Davidson replicas with Shovelhead engines a little over a
decade ago. These models are Touring Glides with
die-cast metal engines and plastic frame and body
components. The wheels revolve, the front end
steers, and the kickstand goes down to allow the
4½" models to stand up.

In 1990, Matchbox released a unique and very
popular item that is a collector's joy—a Harley

Customizing Showroom whose box, made of plastic, folds out and becomes a garage-like showroom. In the box are three small Harleys, signs, and pylons. A great gift idea for the small fry, a great promo piece, and a great collectible.

POETRY IN MOTION

Believe it or not, Harley-Davidson has their own bona-fide troubadour, Martin Jack Rosenblum, who rides the asphalt range on his own Harley in the guise of "The Holy Ranger." Currently, Marty hangs his hat at the Harley-Davidson archives in Milwaukee and serve as the firm's official historian.

A former university professor, this dynamic

Marty Jack Rosenblum, poet, Harley troubadour, and a legendary figure.

"The Holy Ranger," a collection of Harley oriented poems, is a classic out of print collectible, a tribute to the inimitable Harley lifestyle.

motorcycle enthusiast holds a Ph.D. in American literature and lore, history, and culture. In addition, Martin Jack is an established and widely published poet and an essayist on fine art and scholarly subjects. In the 1960's, he was active in the folk-blues revival movement. Rosenblum published a book (illustration) *The Holy Ranger*, a collection of poems. The book is a collectible, fetching up to $25 and now rare and out of print.

BOOKS

The Harley-Davidson Motor Company by David Wright is another essential Harley-sanctioned publication. The original book is a bit outdated and out of print; it will probably be revised somewhere down the line but the first printing of this book is a rarity and valuable.

Another publication of merit and becoming rare originated in-house and is called *The Harley-Davidson Story*. The book, in magazine form, originated in 1989 and is an overview of the history of the V-Twin up to that time, but its eighty pages also include a great deal on the company and is chock

A special Harley issue commemorative piece, The Harley-Davidson Story, *is now a collectible.*

Books like the Peter Reid classic and David Wright's chronological history of the Harley-Davidson Motor Company are collector books, particularly first editions.

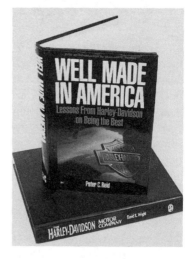

full of photographs. The book was intended as a PR and promotional piece and the fact that it's a special issue makes it all the more valuable.

Other Harley-Davidson Collectible Books:

Motorcycle Collectibles – Leila Dunbar
Shiffer Publishing

Harley-Davidson Sportster – Allan Girdler
Ron Hussey Motorbooks

Harley-Davidson: 1930-1941 – Herbert Wagner
Shiffer Publishing

How to Restore Your Harley – Bruce Palmer
Motorbooks

Harley-Davidson Panheads – Greg Field
Motorbooks

Harley-Davidson Data Book – Rick Connor
Motorbooks

Rebel with a Cause – Gail De Marco
Squarebooks

Harley-Davidson Single & Twin Motorcycles: 1918-1978 – Halward Schrader
Shiffer Publishing

Motorcycle Toys – Sally Gibson
Downes Collector Books

Harley-Davidson, Myth & Mystique –
Randy Leffingwell
Motorbooks

Harley-Davidson Shovelhead – Tom Murphy
Motorbooks

Harley-Davidson Police Motorcycles –
Robert Genat
Motorbooks

Harley-Davidson Electra-Glides –
Malcolm Birkitt
Osprey Automotive

Harley-Davidson 45s – John Carroll
Osprey Automotive

Harley-Davidson – Malcolm Birkitt
Osprey Automotive

Inside Harley-Davidson – Jerry Hatfield
Motorbooks

Harley-Davidson Photographic History –
Wolfgan Wiener
Motorbooks

The Big Book of Harley-Davidson –
Thomas C. Bolfort
Motorbooks

PHOTOGRAPHS

Vintage photographs are regarded as collectibles today and Harley-Davidson oriented photos are no exception. The Harley-Davidson public relations or product photos shown in this book are an exception, for though old and historic, they are not scarce items and can be obtained from the Milwaukee company for a nominal fee. The really rare photos are the ones handed down from generation to generation. Photos showing Granddad on his old Harley or the Harley family with the family two-wheeled vehicle. Pictures of old Harley dealers and dealerships, customers on new vintage Harleys or old riders, competition Harley events. Pictures of older Harley executives, the original Mr. Harley and three Mr. Davidsons, photos of the families and their descendants, these are historic rarities and some old snaps taken by friends and neighbors can be treasures if and when they surface. Those of you

Photos are collectibles. This photo of Willie G., autographed, will be a rare collectible. Willie is a direct descendent of one of the Harley-Davidson founding fathers.

A rare photo shows some Harley riders. The picture is dated August 20, 1950. The photos show Harley racers Kenny Eggers (#59), Larry Hendricks (#87), and Bob Chanes (#20Y). In the background is Tom Sifton, the grandfather of racing cam technology, in a cowboy hat.

who come from two or more generations of Harley folks may find some treasure buried amongst the family photo albums or family photo collection. Personal pictures of older Harleys may also have some merit as well as some value.

Browsing through merchandise at collectible photos meets or flea markets may unearth old photos that may be of interest to a Harley photo collector. The older the photo, the greater its value. A clean photo in mint, unsoiled condition can be a rare find.

ERSATZ HARLEY COLLECTIBLES

There is a gray area in Harley-Davidson collectibles in which the items are Harley-like or Harley-oriented memorabilia. In a roundabout way they are classed among Harley collectibles by Big Twin motorcycle aficionados. I call them ersatz Harley-Davidson collectibles.

To cash in on the desire for Harley products,

A pseudo-Harley Zippo lighter. It can be considered a collectible even though not authorized.

some companies have come up with items like the Zippo lighter shown here. It doesn't say Harley-Davidson, but it does have a pseudo-Harley bike profile and the word "Blockhead," which is a nickname for the newest of Harley V-Twin engines. It's a perfect example of an ersatz collectible. Purists will vie for the actual sanctioned, copyrighted offerings from Harley-Davidson.

Knives are great collectibles and some commemorative issues, not by Harley, are considered motorcycle items and can be offbeat Harley collectibles. The ones with the Harley-Davidson name or logo are the true collectible pieces.

T-shirts...Harley gets ripped off more on ersatz T-shirts than any other item. Traders swarm into Laconia, Daytona, and Sturgis and set up "one-night" stands, selling many illegally printed T-

A Sturgis commemorative buck knife, special issue.

Some T-shirts appear to be Harley issue, but aren't. Bikers do buy and collect them, though, as Harley pieces.

A commemorative Daytona 1993 tank-top. Harley-ites collect these yearly.

shirts which trick the buyers into thinking they have a bona fide Harley shirt. Some shirts are actual Harley issue, backpainted for effect and sales impact. These shirts are not valid collectibles, but collectible because of their unique rarity, definite ersatz examples. Some enterprising T-shirt purveyors actually have specialty T-shirts printed with

An Elvis poster featuring "The King" on a Harley Big Twin. Another pseudo collectible.

copycat Harley bikes or V-Twin engines pictured with minor changes and not a mention of Harley-Davidson to protect the shirtmaker and vendor. Some of these are valid collective pieces and rate high as ersatz T-shirt collectibles. But then, you can go out and buy Japanese V-Twins that seem to be Harley-Davidson clones.

Commemorative bike week T-shirts and tank-tops are valued by Harley rider-collectors even though they are not Harley issue.

Other items can fall into the ersatz category. Take the poster of Elvis Presley. It is strictly an Elvis memorabilia piece, but it says: "Elvis: An American Classic." He is astride a fifties Harley-Davidson, also an American classic. I would definitely class this poster as an ersatz Harley collectible, and one that will be valued by both Elvis and Harley lovers.

SCULPTURES

Sculptures are becoming the hot collectibles. You have Hummels and Lladros, even Walt Disney sculpted pieces.

Cropping up in many a Harley dealership and in the pages of better bike books are magnificent sculptures by Mark Patrick. Patrick sculpts the essence of everything Harley in his pieces, though you don't see a Harley logo anywhere on his masterpieces. Patrick's new release, *Daytona Bound*, shows a rider packing gear for a journey on the road.

The classic sculptures are limited to runs of 1,500 individually numbered pieces, and you will find them if you are lucky at better Harley dealers or motorcycle accessory dealerships. Each one sells for $395 and is well worth the money. Now ersatz in nature, they may be classified as prime Harley collectibles in the future.

Here's an ersatz odd ball, a tour-de-force concept, and a possible future collectible item. It's a box designed in the shape of a V-Twin motor copyrighted in 1994 by Performance Packaging. It's a killer piece showing a V-Twin that has been beautifully rendered on the box.

Three magnificent sculptures by Mark Patrick. Harley-oriented, they are true collectibles.

This box mimics the V-Twin and is a collector oddity.

Brochures like these issued by The Franklin Mint to promote the Harley-Davidson replicas can be potential collectibles.

A rare special limited issue piece, sculpted in porcelain by Hershey Ceramics.

COLLECTIBLE SOURCES

As collectibles, Harley-Davidson items can be easy or hard to find, depending on the piece. Old Harley collectibles, such as early original shirts, jerseys, emblems, patches, oil cans, posters, signage, and catalogs are the rarest of pieces and can be hard to come by.

Old Harley dealers may have accrued some memorabilia through the years, but few will part with these nostalgia items. If they will, it will usually be at the highest prices, for Harley dealers know the value and popularity of old Harley memorabilia.

Many old collectible pieces will surface at motorcycle swap meets and at moderate to high prices depending on the item. Swap meets are run frequently and in all areas of the country, drawing many buyers and sellers. Check local papers or national and regional magazines for times and locations. Swap meets at national gatherings, Daytona, Sturgis, and Laconia, will usually have flea market-type setups and the chances of coming upon items such as old motorcycles, rare parts and engines, tanks, emblems, and T-shirts are good.

You would be surprised at how many Harley-Davidson collectibles surface at antique sales and auctions, since antique dealers know the collectible market and that Harley memorabilia is hot. Yuppies who are Harley riders and have the money for high-ticket collectibles tend to buy up all they can find for both nostalgia and investment purposes. Since antique specialists know collectible values, antique and collectible dealer prices will be on the high side.

Contemporary collectibles or products that are earmarked to become collectibles are easy to find and very accessible in terms of availability and price. Your Harley catalogs and dealerships offer a plethora of collectible and commemorative items. Special pieces such as commemorative knives, watches, belt buckles, and badges are Harley dealer accessory mainstays. Specialty items such as The Franklin Mint collector replica series, sure-fire collectible offerings while the supply lasts, can be obtained via mail order from The Franklin Mint or from its outlets, usually in mall locations throughout the country.

Toy sales and toy collectible auctions and sales will unearth a host of Mattel, Dinky-Toy, Hot Wheels, and old cast iron Hubley Harley-Davidson toy motorcycles.

There are a few accredited sources that will yield much information on Harley collectibles as well as sound information.

Motorcycling Organizations

Antique Motorcycling Club of America
P.O. Box 333
Sweetster, Indiana 46987

American Motorcyclist Association
33 Collegeview Road
Westerville, Ohio 43801

Publications

Hemmings Motor News
Box 390, Rt. 9 West
Bennington, Vermont 05201

Mobilia
RD2, Box 4365
Middlebury, Vermont 05753

Motorcycle Shopper
1353 Herndon Ave
Deltona, Florida 32725

Walneck's Classic Cycle-Trader
923 Janes Ave
Woodridge, Illinois 60571

Motorcycle Collectibles — Direct Sales and Auctions

Dunbar's Gallery
76 Haven Street
Milford, Massachusetts 01757

DISPLAYING COLLECTIBLES

Collectibles may be displayed in any number of accepted ways. Smaller items are best stored in an airtight glass-fronted display case, where they will be well protected from moisture and dirt. This is especially crucial with old cloth and embroidered pieces that almost self-destruct with age and over-handling.

Items such as gas tanks, as shown in this issue, can be framed and hung as dimensional sculptures. Glass-faced collectible display boxes for smaller pieces, available from art and framing shops, will also help to show and protect special items.

Historic photos, magazine ads, and small brochures are best kept in three-hole loose-leaf binders with acetate pocket sheets to protect the fragile surfaces from handling. There are many display boxes available on the art market that are adaptable for storing and presenting collected Harley pieces.

CHAPTER 4

INSTANT EXPERT QUIZ

1. In what year was the original Harley-Davidson motorcycle conceived?

2. What was the first commercially successful Harley-Davidson motorcycle nicknamed?

3. What is the most common official Harley-Davidson logo?

4. What year offered the first Harley-Davidson V-Twins?

5. What new design feature did the company incorporate in 1915?

6. What displacement and how many speeds did the 1915 V-Twins offer?

7. The K model flathead was unveiled in what year?

8. In what year did Harley-Davidson design a bike specifically for police work?

9. How did the European version of the 1927 model J differ from the American version?

10. A rare, pristine 1942 "45" model goes for about how much on the collectible market?

11. What was the first year of the Panhead and how much is it worth in A-1 shape?

12. What was the first Harley-Davidson motorcycle to feature hydraulic front and rear suspension?

13. What rare Panhead model was considered the finest riding machine of its era?

14. What engine considered an engineering milestone followed the Panhead type?

15. From 1936 on, what were the nicknames given to consecutive, major, newly engineered Harley engines?

16. What model Harley-Davidson motorcycle did Elvis Presley own and ride?

17. Who is the "Guru" of modern Harley-Davidson motorcycle design at the factory?

18. How can you tell an authentic Harley collectible item from an implied one?

19. What is the best source for obtaining old and collectible Harley parts and items?

20. Who serves as Harley-Davidson poet and troubadour?

21. What is the name of the book on business and Harley-Davidson written by Peter Reid?

22. Who is the grandfather of Harley racing cam technology?

23. At what four basic annual bike fests can one obtain commemorative T-shirts?

24. What major collectible manufacturing company of today makes replicas of famous Harley motorcycle models?

Answers

1. 1901
2. *The Silent Gray Fellow*
3. *The bar and the shield*
4. 1909
5. *Inlet over exhaust*
6. *61 cu. in. displacement and three speeds*
7. 1915
8. 1907
9. *It had two kick stands; one for the rear wheel, one for the front*
10. *$12,000 and up*
11. *1948 and pristine pieces fetch as much as $23,000*
12. *The 1958, 74 cu. in. FLH Duo-Glide*
13. *The 1960 Electra-Glide*
14. *The Shovelhead*
15. *Knucklehead, Panhead, Shovelhead, Blockhead*
16. *KH*
17. *Willie G. Davidson*
18. *Check for a ©Harley-Davidson stamping on the piece*
19. *Harley-Davidson swap meets*
20. *Martin Jack Rosenblum, the "Holy Ranger"*
21. Well Made in America
22. *Tom Sifton*
23. *Daytona Bike Week, Laconia, Sturgis, Daytona Biketoberfest*
24. *The Franklin Mint*

ABOUT THE AUTHOR

Carl Caiati has been an active motorcyclist and prolific writer covering the subject for the past thirty years.

He has written over twenty-five books on such varied topics as automobiles, motorcycles, art and airbrushing, photography, videography, fishing collectibles, model railroading, and herpetoculture. An acknowledged photographer, his photos and instructional articles have appeared in such magazines as *Popular Mechanics*, *Model Railroader*, *Petersen's Photographic* and *Popular Photography Color Annual*.

His artwork has appeared in *Air Brush Digest*, and he has done a number of technical manuals on airbrushing, some of which have been published in foreign language. At present the author resides in Coral Springs, Florida, where the weather is conducive to his many interests and pursuits.

INDEX